Sagittarius

THIS BOOK BELONGS TO:

_____

THE WONDERFUL WORLD OF ZODIACS

Mimi Jones

Dedicated to all the Sagittarians.

All rights reserved.
No part of this book may be reproduced in any form or by any means, electronic or mechanical, and no photocopying or recording, unless you have written permission from the author.

ISBN 978-1-958985-57-1

Text copyright © 2025 by Mimi Jones

www.joeysavestheday.com

A Mimi Book

WELCOME TO: THE WONDERFUL WORLD OF ZODIACS

SAGITTARIUS

Mimi Jones

Dates:

Sagittarius spans from November 22 to December 21.

Ruling Planet:

Jupiter rules Sagittarius.

Strength:

They are very optimistic and independent.

INDEPENDENT

IMPATIENT

Weakness:
Sagittarians can be impatient and tactless.

Sagittarius

Color:

Their lucky colors are purple, blue, and turquoise.

Lucky Numbers:

3, 7, 9, and 12 are lucky for Sagittarius.

Compatibility:

Sagittarius gets along well with Aries, Leo, Libra, and Aquarius.

Dislikes:

They dislike being constrained and dishonesty.

Likes:

Sagittarians love freedom, travel, and exploring new ideas.

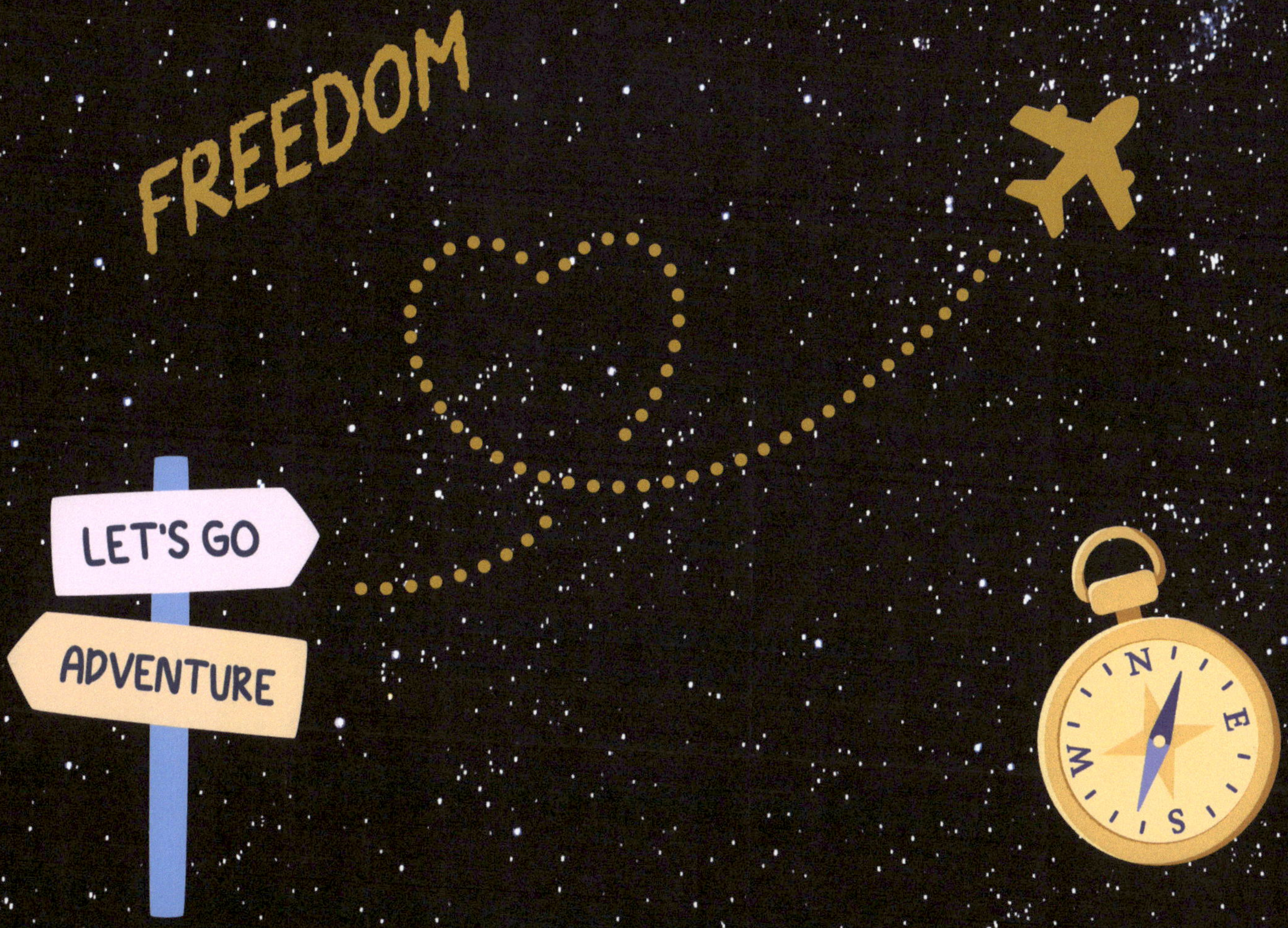

FREEDOM

LET'S GO
ADVENTURE

Career:

They excel in careers that involve travel, teaching, or philosophy.

Positive Trait:

Sagittarians are very open-minded and enthusiastic.

Negative Trait:

Sometimes, they can be a bit too blunt.

Sagittarius

Motto:

Their motto is "I seek."

I
Seek

Favorite Day:

Thursday is their favorite day.

Health:

Sagittarians should take care of their hips and thighs.

Hobbies:

They enjoy traveling, learning, and outdoor adventures.

Famous Sagittarians:

Some famous Sagittarians include Taylor Swift, Brad Pitt, and Winston Churchill.

Style:

They prefer casual, functional, and globally inspired styles.

Challenges:

Sagittarians need to learn to be more patient and considerate of others' feelings.

Friendship:

They are inspiring friends who bring excitement and new perspectives.

Love Life:

In relationships, Sagittarians are passionate and always seeking growth together.

Influence:

They inspire others with their curiosity and zest for life.

Favorite Activities:

Sagittarians love activities that involve learning, exploring, and expanding horizons.

Birthstones:

Topaz and turquoise.

If this Zodiac gem tickled your celestial fancy, then you're in for a treat! Dive into my other Zodiac delights right here:

www.mimibooks.com

THE END!

www.ingramcontent.com/pod-product-compliance
Lightning Source LLC
Chambersburg PA
CBHW040030050426
42453CB00002B/68